HELP IS ON THE WAY

A Child's Book About ADD

Marc A. Nemiroff, PhD
Jane Annunziata, PsyD

Illustrated by Margaret Scott

Magination Press • Washington, DC

Published by
MAGINATION PRESS
An Educational Publishing Foundation Book
American Psychological Association
750 First Street, NE
Washington, DC 20002

Illustrated by Margaret Scott, Washington, DC
Typeset in Bembo and printed by Worzalla Publishing, Stevens Point, WI
Production coordinated by Valerie Montenegro

Library of Congress Cataloging-in-Publication Data
Nemiroff, Marc A.
      Help is on the way : a child's book about ADD / Marc A. Nemiroff,
Jane Annunziata ; illustrated by Margaret Scott.
          p.   cm.
      Summary: Explains the effects of attention deficit hyperactivity
disorder and how it can be handled.
      ISBN 1-55798-505-7 (cb only : acid-free paper)
      1. Attention-deficit hyperactivity disorder—Juvenile literature.
[1. Attention-deficit hyperactivity disorder.]   I. Annunziata,
Jane.   II. Scott, Margaret, ill.   III. Title.
RJ506.H9N45   1998
618.92'8589—dc21   98-3114
                                                                              CIP
                                                                              AC

Manufactured in the United States of America
10 9 8 7 6 5 4 3 2 1

For
Mrs. Gertrude Sherman and Dr. Stan Kulewicz
with gratitude and appreciation

And for
All the children who have
trouble paying attention . . .
Thank you for teaching *us* to
pay attention

What <u>is</u> ADD, anyway?
People talk about it a lot.
(Maybe it's an alphabet game.)

ADD stands for (are you ready? . . . these are BIG words!)

ATTENTION DEFICIT DISORDERS.

THAT MEANS THAT IT IS
HARD TO PAY ATTENTION.

What big words for such simple ideas!

There are lots of different ways to
have trouble paying attention.

WAY NUMBER

You might have trouble sitting still in school or at the dinner table.

Or staying interested in what the teacher is saying.

WAY NUMBER

Or, your hands and feet might work before your brain is finished telling them what to do.

OR, YOU MIGHT SAY THINGS QUICKLY THAT YOU DIDN'T REALLY WANT TO SAY.

5

Or, you might have trouble paying attention to how other kids feel.

WAY NUMBER

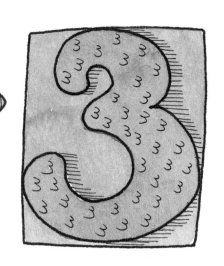

You might have trouble being organized. . . . That means knowing what to do next when there is a lot to do.

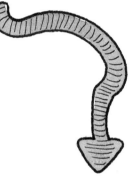

(It also means keeping your toys or school supplies just neat enough to be able to find them when you want them.)

Sometimes it's hard to remember things.

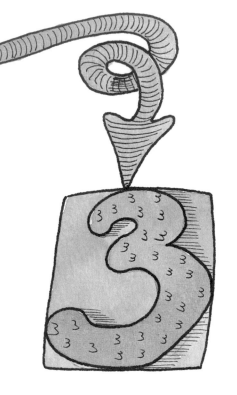

Numbers 1, 2, and 3 are different KINDS of ADD.
(That's why we call them ADDs . . . because there are different kinds.)

Even though they are different, they can all make kids feel the same way...

And sometimes kids have other feelings, too:

BUT

There are lots of different helpers:

EVERYBODY

gets help in
different ways,

BUT...

here is
how it
often
happens:

Teachers or parents notice a problem. (Kids often think that something is wrong, too, but they don't know what it is.)

Then your parents call a doctor or other kind of special helper.

These helpers have very big names, and they are very important. They need pages of their own!

ediatrician:

This is your regular doctor, for checkups and when you feel sick.

She can get the ball rolling to help find out if you have ADD.

Psychologist.

He does special activities that are a little like the things you do at school.

Psychologists are feelings doctors, too. That means they are also therapists.

18

Therapist

She helps you figure out your feelings, worries, and things that bother you because of ADD. Many children with ADD need therapists who can be a special "feelings friend." The therapist will also help your parents know how to help you.

Neurologist:

This doctor knows a lot about how the brain works. (And the brain is in charge of how we think and feel and behave.) He helps us learn more about ADDs.

We forgot to tell you—your brain is inside your head, up between your ears.

Brain

You might go to one or more of these helpers.

These helpers
figure out together
whether you really have
ADD.

We've got it!
It's an
ADD!

Even though all these helpers do different things to figure this out, they all agree on one thing, one VERY IMPORTANT thing.

(It's the most important idea in this book.)

Are You Ready!

23

ADD is . . .
NOT YOUR FAULT.

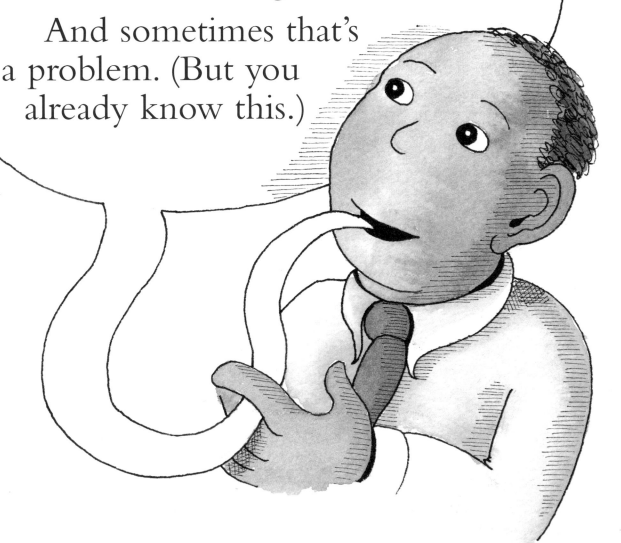

ADD comes from how the brain works. Nobody's positive yet just what happens inside the brain, but they are sure that kids didn't <u>make</u> it happen!

In ADD, the brain works a little differently. Sometimes it feels as if it works too fast; sometimes it feels as if it doesn't work fast enough.

And sometimes that's a problem. (But you already know this.)

"I'm working so HARD!"

29

Well, to begin with, there are two places where (almost) EVERYONE gets help.

At home ~ 🏠 ~ you and your family ~ 👪 ~ will learn how to get things done with less arguing.

You ~ 😊 (ME?) ~ will learn how to do things one step at a time.

And your mom and dad will learn how to be a good coach. (Others can be coaches, too.)

COACH FLUFFY

COACH BABY SITTER

COACH DAD

COACH MOM

COACH GRANDMA

A coach is someone who teaches you how to do better, and who cheers you on when you get discouraged.

Then <u>everyone</u> starts to feel better, and **you** will start to know that you <u>can</u> do things well.

33

2. At school  your teacher will find a way to guide your attention so you can learn important things.

You will learn how to put the brakes on better when you need to.

THAT MEANS LEARN TO STOP YOURSELF WHEN YOU NEED TO.

You will learn how to listen to other kids and how to take turns and then playing GOES BETTER.

and then...

School is more

Some children get other kinds of help, too.

EXTRA
THE A.D.D. TIMES
IT ALL DEPENDS ON WHAT THEY NEED, AND EVERY CHILD IS DIFFERENT.

More Helps

HELP IS ON THE WAY

MEDICINE

THERAPY

TUTORING

Sometimes medicine helps children pay attention better.

Sometimes it helps them calm down.

LOTS of children think that medicine is a BIG help.

Therapy can be a **BIG** help, too.

There are different kinds of therapy.

PLAY THERAPY

GROUP THERAPY

FAMILY THERAPY

BEHAVIOR THERAPY

In play therapy, you play and talk.
That's how you understand your
feelings about having ADD.

When you understand your feelings
about ADD, the problems get smaller.

GROUP THERAPY

In group therapy, several children meet together with the therapist. In the group, you play and take part in activities while you learn good ways to make friends and get along at home and at school.

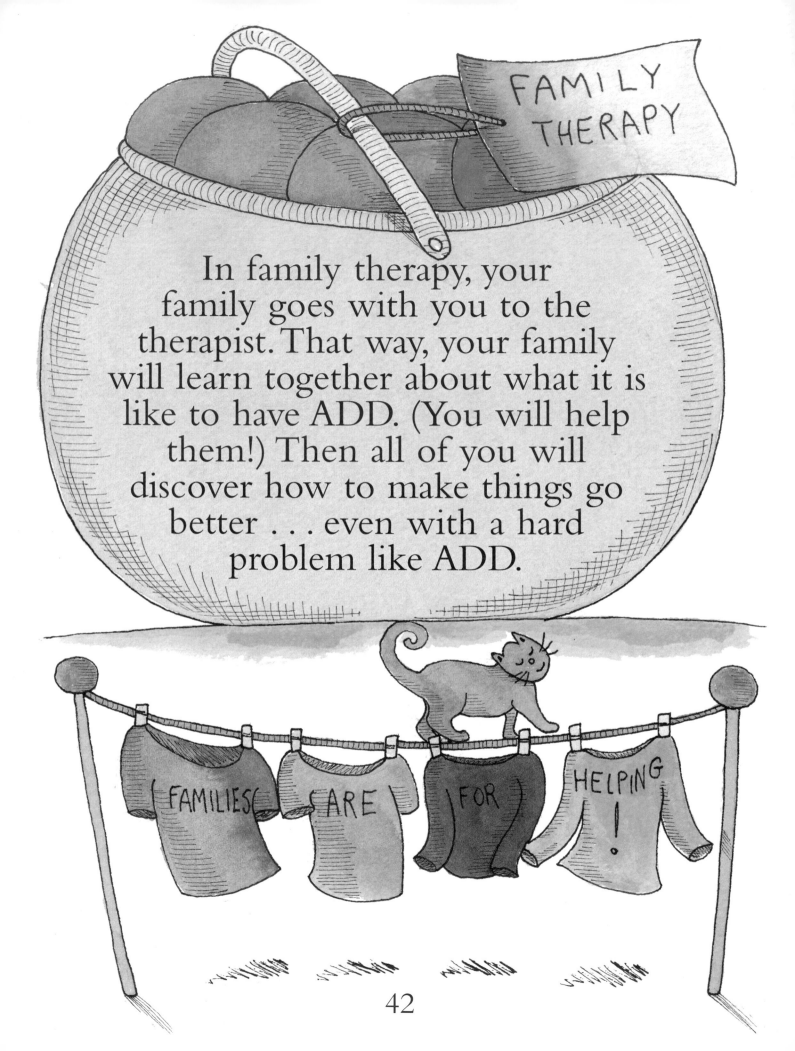

In family therapy, your family goes with you to the therapist. That way, your family will learn together about what it is like to have ADD. (You will help them!) Then all of you will discover how to make things go better . . . even with a hard problem like ADD.

In behavior therapy, the therapist works with your behaviors (those are the things you do that are problems at school, at home, and with friends). The therapist teaches you and your parents ways to make problem behaviors not be big problems anymore. Sometimes they use charts with stars and other stickers.

43

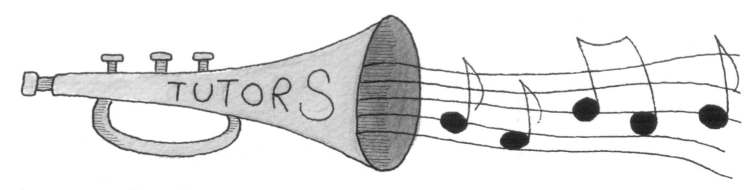

can help, too.
(Tutors are like teachers,
but just for YOU.)

They work . . .

Tutors teach you how to learn . . . because some things can be harder to learn than others.

these "helps" work in different ways . . . but they all get to the same place. . . . Kids start feeling better about themselves and doing better at home and school.

ONE LAST THING...

Kids don't usually think of this

&

it can help when you feel dis-couraged (like wanting to give up).

49

When you

and get the

the good
things
about you
SHINE
through.

FOR PARENTS AND GUARDIANS

The purpose of this book is to help children 5 to 9 years old (and their parents) understand the attention deficit disorders (ADDs). We have tried to capture, from the child's point of view, the experience of an ADD. As such, the book is not intended as a comprehensive text or guidebook. The following comments are intended to serve as a review of the fundamentals of the ADDs, placed here to enhance your use of the book with your child.

ADDs are a cluster of several problems with attention. We find that it is useful to think of three differing aspects of attentional problems. These are:

- Attention problems associated with **hyperactivity,** or attention deficit hyperactivity disorder (ADHD). This means that a child has difficulty paying attention because of an excessive level of activity.

- Attention problems associated with **lack of impulse control.** Here, the child has trouble with many aspects of self-control, resulting in diminished ability to pay attention.

- Attention problems associated with **poor organizational capacity.** This refers to a difficulty staying organized, such as knowing what to do next, in a variety of situations. Thus, the child is not able to focus attention in a productive way.

It is important to distinguish when these attentional problems are truly an attention deficit *disorder*, as opposed to when they are related to other factors. These other factors might be *psychological* (e.g., anxiety, stress, oppositional behaviors, or other ongoing emotional problems), *temperamental* (e.g., an inborn activity level that is higher than average), or *developmental* (e.g., differing activity levels and tolerance for sustained attention at different ages).

Some additional examples might be helpful to clarify what we mean. A young child who naturally enjoys being active and prefers to be up and about rather than sitting still (e.g., at a school desk) is not necessarily an ADD child. (These children, when in the lower grades at school, may sometimes be incorrectly identified as having attentional problems when they are simply being active youngsters.) Similarly, an unusually anxious youngster may manifest his distress through behaviors that are similar to those of ADD children. For these anxious children, the principal problem is emotionally based (anxiety) rather than an ADD, and the preferred treatment is quite different. Thus, a carefully considered diagnostic workup is in order before assuming that a child has an ADD or before labeling a child with this diagnosis.

SYMPTOMS OF THE ATTENTION DEFICIT DISORDERS

Examples of **hyperactivity** include:

- Excessive activity level resulting in fidgeting, squirming, or difficulty sitting still. This might occur at home, in a movie theater, or in the classroom.

- Difficulty staying focused on one thing for any length of time because of the child's excessive activity level. Thus, ideas do not get developed well; flitting from play activity to play activity occurs, leaving a mess in the child's wake; the child has difficulty staying still long enough to complete an assignment or a chore.

- Difficulty managing oneself in the physical environment. This refers to the child's difficulty moving his body smoothly in space. The child may appear clumsy, bumping into doors, walls, or furniture. There may also be more than the usual amount of spilled milk, dropped glasses, or silverware on the floor.

Lack of impulse control refers to:

- Having trouble waiting or listening. This can result in interrupting others or speaking before thinking. The child may also have difficulty tolerating a long wait in line, waiting for a parent's help, and so on.

- Being impatient. The child may be impatient about taking turns or may grab a toy away from another child because it is too hard to wait for it. This is an *impatience* problem rather than a true *sharing* problem.

- Difficulty tolerating frustration. Thus, the child may demonstrate an unpredictable "flashpoint" (loss of temper) or may appear to shift arbitrarily from one activity to another. A child may seem uninterested in certain activities, but he or she may actually be frustrated with mastering those activities rather than truly uninterested.

- An attraction to "daredevil" activities. The child's need for excitement (which may be greater than other children's) and his or her lack of self-control override good sense about safety.

Poor organizational capacity[1] refers to:

- Becoming overwhelmed, frustrated, or discouraged by complex tasks that have several steps, even though other children of the same age do not find the tasks too difficult or complicated. Examples include asking an 8-year-old to do homework, put the schoolbooks away, and then set the table for dinner; or asking a 4-year-old to "clean your room" (which would actually include putting dirty laundry in a basket, placing toys in a bin, and putting stuffed animals on the bed). Sometimes the child cannot remember all the steps, and sometimes the child cannot come up with the steps in a broad task. The child may also have difficulty knowing where to begin.

- Having difficulty following directions, whether they are spoken or written.

- Experiencing marked difficulty making the transition from one activity or idea to another. This might be noted in kindergarten as a refusal to join circle time or, at any age, as a difficulty ending one activity and starting another. Children with this problem may also become distressed with other types of transitions (or changes), such as a new furniture arrangement, a new paint color in the house, a change in the order of events during a school day, and so on.

- A tendency toward distractibility—that is, a difficulty maintaining focus on the task at hand. This makes children more apt to lose things, become forgetful, or lose track of where they are in their thought process or what they are in the middle of doing at the moment.

---

[1] The term *executive functions* is sometimes used when discussing organizational capacity. This refers to the child's ability to conceptualize what he needs to do and in what order he needs to do it. It is like having a secretary in your mind. For ADD children, it is as if the secretary is "out to lunch"!

- Becoming first excited but then overwhelmed by an environment that is highly stimulating, such as a room with many people and much activity.

DIAGNOSIS OF THE ADDs

It is very important that a careful diagnosis be made by qualified professionals, such as child psychologists or psychiatrists, pediatric neurologists, or pediatricians. Diagnosing is usually a process (rather than a single appointment) during which a professional will consult with you, interview your young child (sometimes in a playroom), obtain information from relevant people involved with your child (e.g., teachers, day care providers), and synthesize all of this information. Often, you and your child's teachers will also be asked to fill out a behavioral checklist to aid in the process. This much care is necessary so that the final diagnosis is accurate and has ruled out other possible diagnoses. [Of course, it is also possible that a diagnosis of an ADD can coexist with (a) emotional problems such as anxiety or depression or (b) problems with behavior separate from the ADD-related behaviors.]

LIVING WITH THE ADD CHILD

The first thing to keep in mind regarding your ADD youngster is that your child is not "being bad," that is, not misbehaving intentionally. Rather, your child has an ADD that causes some of the problems that resemble intentional misbehavior. Actually, ADD children usually are working very hard to do their best, stay in control, and pay attention. They also may try to stay away from situations in which they know they cannot do their best. Examples are a youngster who knows he cannot sit still in church, so he announces that he does not feel well enough to go, and a child who does not join others on the playground at recess because she knows that a problem relating with other children may occur. These children need understanding, patience, and structure from their parents. Punishment of an ADD child for ADD-based behaviors is rarely appropriate (or effective).

Another thing to keep in mind is the puzzling way that these children might respond to input (stimulation) from their environment. On the one hand, they tend to get overly excited (or "jazzed-up") when the environment is too stimulating for them. Examples are a room with bright lights and filled with people and loud music, and a very busy classroom environment in which various activities are occurring simultaneously (and noisily). On the other hand—and this is the puzzling part—sometimes these children crave action or stimulation and can tolerate and even enjoy it more than the "average" child can. Thus, they can play a home video game while listening to a story on tape and be able to focus reasonably effectively on both. We feel that it is important to mention this because it is something that is curious and confusing to parents, and it runs counter to what logic would lead us to expect.

Once your child has been diagnosed with an ADD, you will need to learn to become an advocate for him in several areas (e.g., school, day care, recreational activities, after-school programs). Primarily, you will need to speak with those people who work with or take care of your child to explain the concept of ADD and what ADD means for him. Primarily, you will need to help them understand the nature of your child's difficulties and that he does not "misbehave" or fail to pay attention in order to be "difficult." Then you can help his teachers, sitters, and others devise strategies that will guide and help your child to manage himself better each day. You should monitor your child's progress regularly, discussing how things are going. *Reminder: Advocacy is an ongoing process; it does not end.* It is more than simply informing relevant people a single time about your child's ADD. It requires regular conferences and continual attention to how your child is doing and what can be done to help him. This is partly because the things that need to be done to help the ADD child are ever-shifting.

Just as you will be an advocate for your child at school, you will need to help your family understand the nature of your youngster's difficulties. It is useful to explain the child's ADD to brothers and sisters and the extended family members. Then they can come to see the youngster not as a problem, but rather as someone who needs their support. A supportive and understanding family then becomes the necessary environment for the ADD youngster to improve her behavior. Family therapy is often helpful here. In addition, you might consider talking with members of your extended family so that they, too, can understand her better (and, as it applies, be less critical of her).

There are numerous ways that you can be helpful to your child at home. Children with one of the ADDs usually respond well to certain accommodations at home. For example, a disorganized young child who cannot find her clothes in the morning will appreciate picture labels on her dresser drawers showing her what is inside each one. Labeling also may work for helping a child learn how to clean her room. Establishing and maintaining regular morning and bedtime rituals also help (e.g., an evening routine of first bath, then tooth brushing, then story, then bed). To help your child make an easier transition from one activity to another, or from being at home to leaving the house, alert her 5 to 10 minutes in advance of the impending shift in activity, and then again 2 to 3 minutes before. In addition, it is useful to provide step-by-step directions for complex tasks. These should usually be stated one at a time. When getting a younger child ready to leave the house, you might say, "First put away your just-played-with toys, then put on your coat, then your gloves; now let's go to the car." For somewhat older children, the same principles apply, but on a somewhat more developmentally mature level. As you come to understand just how ADD is manifesting itself in *your* child, you will invent your own ways of providing structure at home.

A Note About Homework

Most children need help in organizing their homework and in getting it done. Often they can become overwhelmed by assignments, regardless of how simple they may seem. You can help by ordering the assignments, saying, for example, "There are three assignments today: Which would you like to do first? Spelling? OK. Let's do the first five words. Good. Here are the next five words. . . [etc.]. Now it's time for arithmetic. . . [etc.]." Likewise, children get visually overwhelmed by too much material on a single page (this is especially true of arithmetic problems). Your child is likely to appreciate it (although not say so!) if you either (a) use a blank piece of paper to block out all but the single problem he is working on or (b) rewrite the problems, placing only two or three on each page. Again, these are just some examples for helping your child. As you work with him, you will develop your own techniques, geared to your own child.

A Note About Keeping Charts

Many parents (and sometimes teachers) find it useful to use a charting system to help their ADD children regulate and monitor their behaviors. Usually the chart looks like a monthly or weekly blank calendar (weekly may be better for the youngest ADD children). The chart is used only for specific, targeted behaviors, such as doing homework. After the homework is done for the day, for example, a gold star sticker is put in the blank box for that day. When the child accumulates enough stars, then he can receive a reward. Sometimes, after a while, the gold stars themselves become the reward. The reward should come after a reasonably attainable number of stars, or "good days." This might be (at first) a week during which the gold stars outnumber the non-gold star boxes for a given week. Then perhaps the reward should come after five gold stars in a row, and so on. *Reminder: While charting is often helpful, it is important to use the chart for a* limited *number of targeted behaviors.* Otherwise, the process of charting itself becomes problematic. In our experience, charting loses its usefulness after the initial weeks or months. Therefore, it is important to do it well from the beginning. A child psychologist (or sometimes your pediatrician) can help you learn more about charting and other behavioral approaches.

Your child's teachers can also find ways to alter their approach to her so that she can manage herself better and learn more efficiently in the classroom. You should be involved in, and informed about, the development of schoolroom strategies. That way, you and your child's teachers can be approaching your ADD youngster in compatible, complementary ways.

SOME THOUGHTS ABOUT MEDICATION

Medication is frequently used as a treatment for the ADDs. It is often effective, sometimes dramatically so. But remember, the medication is not *curing* your child's ADD. Rather, it is, through its chemistry, altering your child's ability to manage hyperactivity, impulse control, and organizational tasks. The medication therefore needs to be considered as an *ongoing improver of your child's ability to function with his ADD. Reminder: It is essential to adhere to the dosage and administration schedule as prescribed by the pediatrician or child psychiatrist.* Do not alter the dosage, times of administration, or frequency of administration of your child's medication without consulting the prescribing physician. The prescribing physician should also be informed about side effects or changes in the effectiveness of the medication over time. There are also children who respond well to treatment interventions without the use of medication.

THOUGHTS ABOUT PLAY THERAPY

In our experience, play therapy is often a useful adjunctive approach to help children with ADDs. Quite often, ADDs bring with them important negative effects on children's self-esteem, their sense of their own worthiness, and their ability to manage in the world of friends. There is often, too, anxiety associated with performance (in varieties of tasks at school, at home, and socially). Children often believe that they somehow brought the ADD on themselves, or that it is otherwise their fault. They can become locked into provocative, negative behaviors as a way of seeking to prove how unworthy or "bad" they are. Play therapy addresses these issues through techniques of interactive and interpreted play between your child and his therapist. Young children express their underlying concerns, their worries, their fantasies, their wishes for mastery, their fears, and their opinions about themselves primarily through play. They do not look to language the way older children and adults do. A trained play therapist uses your child's play as a guide and helps him become more aware of what worries him. The play therapist also works with parents, usually in separate sessions, to help them understand their child's concerns better. The play therapy environment can also be helpful in pointing behavioral patterns out to a child and helping him develop and try more appropriate alternatives.

THOUGHTS ABOUT OCCUPATIONAL THERAPY AND THE USE OF TUTORS

There are some ADD children who require, and improve with, occupational therapy. The occupational therapist works with specially designed equipment in a highly active fashion. These techniques can help children develop a better sense of their own bodies and how they work, as well as provide strengthening of more poorly developed muscle systems. Youngsters then may feel that they have greater mastery over their own bodies and their movements. Young children can be very responsive to occupational therapy; they tend to like the activities.

Some ADD children work well with tutors. A tutor can be effective in several ways: (a) actually helping your child with her homework; (b) helping your child learn how to approach homework, regardless of content, and *how* to study; and (c) helping your child learn strategies that improve organizational skills.

We hope that you and your child find this little book helpful. We have worked hard to try to have the ADD child feel understood as he or she reads it (or has it read to him or her). The language is as simplified as we could make it. There are many books written for parents that speak *about* the ADDs. We hope we have written a book that speaks *to* ADD children.

A final comment: We know that it can be challenging, and at times difficult, to be the parent of an ADD child. Parenting under the best of circumstances is not easy. Parenting an ADD child often requires extra energy, patience, and fortitude. We hope that this book will help you through the difficult moments. When the going gets rough, it also helps to remember that ADD children also bring something special into our lives—enthusiasm, energy, an abundance of ideas, and a zest for life. As you learn about and help your ADD child, you will have the pleasure of watching your child make the most of these wonderful traits.

Marc Nemiroff, PhD
Jane Annunziata, PsyD

About the Authors and the Illustrator

Marc A. Nemiroff has a PhD in clinical psychology from the Catholic University of America. He is Core Faculty on the Infant and Early Childhood Mental Health Program at the Washington School of Psychiatry, and Clinical Faculty at the George Washington University Doctor of Psychology program. Dr. Nemiroff is an affiliate member of the Baltimore-Washington Society for Psychoanalysis. He has worked with children and their families in various clinical settings for many years. Dr. Nemiroff maintains a private practice in Potomac, Maryland. He is coauthor, with Jane Annunziata, of *A Child's First Book About Play Therapy* (1990) and *Why Am I an Only Child?* (1998).

Jane Annunziata has a PsyD in clinical psychology from Rutgers University. She has taught at the University of Bergen (Norway), Mary Washington College, and George Mason University. She currently is adjunctive Clinical Faculty in the George Washington University PsyD program. She has coauthored *A Child's First Book About Play Therapy* (with Marc Nemiroff, 1990), *Solving Your Problems Together: Family Therapy for the Whole Family* (with Phyllis Jacobson-Kram, 1994), and *Why Am I an Only Child?* (with Marc Nemiroff, 1998). Her videotape demonstration, *Play Therapy With a Six-Year-Old* (1998), is part of the APA Psychotherapy Videotape Series II. She previously was a member of the Woodburn CMHC Children's Intensive Treatment Team in northern Virginia. Dr. Annunziata maintains a private practice specializing in work with children and families in McLean, Virginia.

Margaret Scott is a prizewinning children's book illustrator. She has illustrated books for the U.S. Department of Education, Reading Is Fundamental, and the American Psychological Association, among others. Ms. Scott has done work in pen-and-ink, watercolor, and colored pencil for such clients as the National Association for the Education of Young Children, UNICEF, the Children's Defense Fund, the National Conference of Mayors, and *Smithsonian* Magazine. Ms. Scott divides her time between her Washington, DC studio and her 150-year-old house in the historic village of Quantico on Maryland's Eastern Shore.